FUELLED BY **FEAR**

MOTLALEPULE MOKHINE

FUELLED BY **FEAR**

INSPIRED
PUBLISHING

Fuelled By Fear
First Edition, First Impression 2019
978-0-6398256-0-1
Copyright © Motlalepule Mokhine

Published by:
Inspired Publishing
PO Box 82058 | Southdale | 2135
Johannesburg , South Africa
Email: info@inspiredpublishing.co.za
www.inspiredpublishing.co.za

Short Stories
Fuelled By Fear

ACKNOWLEDGEMENTS

I am thankful and give all the glory to God above. It is through Him, that this book has seen the light. I am truly grateful.

My late parents, Keti and Nosisi Mokhine, for loving me unconditionally My friend and business partner Nomvuyo Bengane, for the partnership in the work around fear and your overall support.

My son, family, friends and colleagues, who have been an amazing support in my life.

All my life teachers, formal and informal.

INTRODUCTION

'If you hear a voice within you say you cannot paint, then by all means paint, and that voice will be silenced'. Vincent Van Gogh

When I started business, after years in corporate, I met with someone I always looked up to, someone I consider a mentor. I was excited to share my news with him. He told me in no uncertain terms that I would not make it. He told me that the business of coaching, which is what I was getting into, is difficult. He said I didn't have the right contacts that can help me get setup and settled in this industry. He felt sorry for me.

I was rattled, but I decided, 'to go ahead and paint'.
This book is about celebrating my story: my story of breaking free from fear, of silencing the voice of fear. My story of having to look fear in the face, and courageously declare, 'I will carry on painting'.
I am pleased that you have the book in your hands. My hope is that it helps you get, inspired to go on, despite fear or anxiety - you too can live a life where fear ceases to paralyse you.

I am sharing with you some of the frightful realities I have had to confront - stories that I was fearful to share, from my fear of shame, to insecurities around my body as well as what has shaped me and some of my quirkiness.

My past and my character seem contradictory. I was raised by strong assertive parents yet I suffered low-self-esteem which, I think, I managed to hide very well. I suffered from a massive case of fear. Fear of showing up, fear of sharing my opinion, fear of speaking first.
This book for me, is about stepping up and out. It is about embracing all my strengths, beauty and power. It is about allowing myself to be noticed.

#Iknowthisfosho

FEAR can be a great ally towards *discovering one's own strength*. **FEAR** does *not* have to oppress or paralyse. Triumphing over **FEAR** is doable *I matter and I am much loved*

NOMAHLUBI

02:10am, is generally a time of deep sleep for most people. It was comfortably dark and peaceful or so she thought. It was not uncommon in the township to be hearing screams or people running away from seeming danger in the middle of the night. As usual, Nomahlubi was awakened by such noises. She would sit up, wondering whose child that was, running for their dear life. Previously, she would tiptoe to the window hoping to see some activity and she stopped doing that because of the helplessness that overwhelmed her.

She would be lying in bed, her husband next to her oblivious of what she was experiencing. He often tried to shut the noise out to get as much rest and sleep because he would have to be up at 04h00 to prepare for work. Every morning after such an event, she would relate to the children how there were people running in the street. There were instances where there would be a fatal stabbing not too far from her house. The townships have always been violent.

This is the environment in which she and her husband were raising their children. These experiences could potentially breed massive fear or violence in the children. There is an amazing way in which they managed as parents to almost insulate their children away from the fear of the violence that was prevalent in the township.

Nomahlubi was a strong woman who had survived tough times. Her goal in life was to support and protect her family, as well as instil strong family values to steer her children away from the danger characteristic of life in the township. Church played a big role in crafting the values that were the opposite of violence and fear.

She was a working mother and often coming back from work she would sit down for a cup of tea and, if needed, go out for some errands. Her usual practice was to go relax on her bed after work, sometimes having her tea brought to her.

Nomahlubi had an interesting relationship with her bed. Her bed represented comfort, a retreat, love, a place to go refresh and gain strength. Whenever she felt emotional about anything, her bed was her refuge. It felt as though it had the ability to soothe and comfort her. Same as when she was tired, retreating to her bed would somehow restore and rejuvenate her.

Born in Matatiele, Nomahlubi grew up in what is now Mpumalanga, where her parents had settled. Her father was a church minister and, as a result, they moved house often. She was sickly as a child. As a baby, she spent most days in a cardboard box in the kitchen until she was a toddler. This was so that her mother would be able to watch her throughout – moving the cardboard box everywhere in the house she went. Older children would push her around and that should have had the same effect as being wheeled in a pram. At that time prams were not affordable to most black families unless they were hand me downs from the white people they worked for. Her mother would sing lullabies and hymns to her as she moved from one room to the other. Nomahlubi was also baptized inside the cardboard box at home because she was too sick to be taken to church on the day. She had been so sickly growing up that there was little hope that she would live past the age of two.

God was gracious to her in that she grew up and started school but due to ill health, she was away from school a lot, so much so that, it made little sense to continue with school.

She got a reprieve in her early adult stage, got married, settled and had five children. Even though she had settled in the township with her family, full of violence, breeding fear, she was very protective of her children and had created an imaginary bubble, where they were contained.

Since she lived her life almost with an awareness of how close she had danced with death as a child, Nomahlubi loved life and loved people. She had nothing to worry about, if things were fine in the present. People around her enjoyed her immensely because she liked to please. Her community knew that she was committed to make them happy, often at great cost to herself. Her lifestyle demonstrated her extravagance and larger than life persona. She always had a reason to celebrate. For someone who was not expected to live longer than two years, it made sense that she experienced life as a continuous celebration: something that the family got to understand much later. At the end of every year her children would receive gifts for passing their exams, there would be a celebratory lunch for a good year, and so it went on. The initial intention with most of these lunches would be to keep them small, for family only. No one ever understood how they ended up with more than just family present. Nomahlubi was never bothered by that. Her nature allowed her to get away with all these because she was relentless in proving that, there was always a reason to celebrate.

Sitting up on her bed after work, with her cigarette and a cup of weak tea, one could just see from the look on her face when she was deep in thought. Her soft eyes would be gazing into the distance with her head tilted to the side. Her room was beautiful. She was very particular about the co-ordination in every room, the colours and make of the furniture items. She lived in a township four roomed house which was very clean, organised and wonderfully done. Cleanliness was important to her and she also had good organisational skills. "Absolutely no clutter" was her motto. She believed in order, regardless of whether the room was accessible to outsiders or not.

Despite being sickly as a child Nomahlubi grew up to become a very heavy smoker, smoking about ten cigarettes a day and indulged in alcohol, sometimes a lot. She refused to see the relationship between her health and smoking. It almost seemed like she knew that she would not live long, that is why her life was a celebration throughout. She never worried or tried to fit in the stereotypes of what a woman was supposed to be like –

she chose to do what she wanted to do whenever she wanted to do it.

"Let me sit down and think about this matter", she would say whenever there was a matter to be dealt with, before she settled into her bed, with a cigarette. Black tea and a cigarette were part of her thinking ritual.

It is almost impossible to count the number of times people tried to talk her out of smoking and drinking alcohol. Her justification was that we all are going to die, smokers and non-smokers alike. This would be said with so much attitude that no one would be brave enough to raise this matter for the second time.
Nomahlubi embraced the contradictions of her life gracefully. A very committed Christian and church member in a leadership position; she never allowed her drinking and smoking to define her relationship with God. She was at peace with how she had defined and carved her spirituality.

Her nature and tendency of being "Madame Speaker" of the house endeared her to most. This was demonstrated whenever there was a need to confront someone or give instructions. She would retreat to her bed and call the person into the bedroom, no matter what time of the day it was. From the tone of her voice, they would know what to anticipate. When they walked into her bedroom, they would sheepishly look into her eyes to assess her state and mood. Nomahlubi had big bold eyes and would look you in the eyes when interacting. Whenever she was upset or angry, her eyes seemed to become even bigger than normal. That was intimidating to some people.

At different times, when in a good mood, the family members would be summoned to her bedroom, for fellowship and bonding. Often this would be on a Saturday or Sunday afternoon when everyone was back from their shopping sprees or visiting with friends. The tone and pattern of these meetings was relaxed and jovial. Those indeed were pleasant times.

Her bed had become a very significant anchor for her. She felt very strong and in control whenever she was in her bed. She also would be vulnerable, during moments when she was not well. Events and news had an interesting way of altering her state. She could be unwell, lying on her bed and taking time to "listen to her pain", as she always said, and someone could say something that jolted her to action. She would change instantly, and she would take charge like a bull in a ring.

She showed her soft side, when her teenage daughter, was dealing with issues of identity, body issues, and rejection. She rose up to the occasion, comforting her daughter, assuring her that she was still young and had a whole future ahead of her. She encouraged her to focus on her future.

When her son's girlfriend became pregnant, she was disappointed at the timing. Her response was that he would have to marry the girl before the baby arrived. He did not object.

She took charge and started with preparations for her son's wedding. This was very interesting in their household. In the African tradition, it is the uncles and aunts, sometimes the father too that goes to the woman's family to negotiate lobola, (dowry). Nomahlubi was not going to allow these negotiations to happen without her being there. She made the appointment with the girlfriend's parents and agreed with her husband that the two of them would be the one's going to negotiate. The two of them went for the initial meeting and it culminated in a beautiful wedding for her son.

After the wedding, it was back to the "boardroom," the bedroom with Nomahlubi on her bed and her daughters for a post-mortem of the event. It was all girly, reviewing, the clothes, the food and other related matters. Overall, they all agreed that it had been a good celebration.

It was such a contrast, when she was unwell on her bed because when she was "in action" her emotional strength, wisdom and chutzpah would be on display. She would walk with confidence and speak with clarity. Her deep, good voice worked in her favour; she would have done well on radio. Her eye contact was almost intimidating, and she liked that – she enjoyed intimidating others, men and women alike.

Her siblings embraced her irrepressible nature. They had developed their own ways of coping with her demanding self. They were strong personalities themselves who found it easier to bow to her whims rather than challenge her. On the other side, she used to laugh a lot with her siblings and others around her. On her bed, she looked relaxed, in control and at her peak. She felt safe as well. She used to share stories of her growing up, with the family. In one instance, they were planning a journey by train to a relative in the Mpumalanga. "A journey by train, from Johannesburg to Ermelo takes the whole night," she told them.

"Firstly, you prepare the food, for your travel the day before; dumpling, a whole chicken as well as cool drinks and snacks.' This was going to be a long journey. 'You also make sure that your bags are packed the night before so that you are free the next day for any last-minute errands. Late in the afternoon, you board a taxi that takes you to the Johannesburg station. Once you get there, you listen for an announcement to inform you at which platform the train to Ermelo will be – it was often on platform 13. Once there, you would wait until the train arrives. The long distant trains were different from the local trains that travelled from home to Johannesburg. This long-distance train had benches that converted into beds. And if you were in second class, which was more expensive, you would get more luxury, by way of blankets and meal. First class was for whites only, she told them. They looked at her, absorbing every word she said, with their eyes glued on her every movement and detail. This train normally arrived at Ermelo station the next morning at 06:30am. There would be an announcement to inform all the passengers that the train is approaching Ermelo station and you would pack your stuff and prepare yourself to alight. The cherry on top would be when your hosts are waiting for you at the station. After that enchanting narration, the children couldn't wait to travel to Ermelo.

A lot of planning happened on that bed too. Nomahlubi was chairperson of the local women's group and sometimes she would sit and brainstorm challenges she faced in this group with her daughters.

Even though ill health continued to plague her, she displayed strength especially when she had to deal with something. In moments when she was not well, she would go lie down on her bed. Her bed received her warmly always, making her feel like a baby in a mother's womb. Looking at her lying on that bed had some serenity and innocence about it. She made sure she took advantage of opportunities to teach and inform her children. They once had a discussion on the death penalty, the children asking her who was responsible to kill the people sentenced to death. She related what she had heard. The fact that there was an electric chair where people would be killed, and that there was also hanging. There were stories that on the eve of someone being executed they would be asked what meal they wanted for their last day. Whatever their choice of meal would be, they would be served that, as a last meal. They were also allowed visitation by family giving them an opportunity to bid each other goodbye. It felt grim.

She imagined her bed as a multipurpose place where she was able to access everything that she needed. If she desired to be in a park, on a late summer afternoon, this bed turned into a park and provided the atmosphere of a park. There she imagined herself with her grandchildren, and a picnic basket enjoying the sun. She went into memory, remembering when as a toddler, she would be sitting comfortably in a cardboard next to the coal stove on a winter day, feeling very warm and cared for.

This bed was tailor-made to take her troubles away. It had memory, intuition and different imaginary accessories. Whenever she had a headache, she would get into bed and in a few minutes, lavender oil smells would permeate her head. The bed would massage her temples gently, sending her off to sleep only to awaken later, without the headache. When it was her blood pressure that shot up, the bed would know, just by her getting inside. It would massage her entire body, getting her to relax, lowering the blood pressure. Whenever she felt depressed, the family would offer her anti-depressant tea, three times a day for a week and get her to relax. This would be a week where she would lay low and the family would give her the space she needs.

In her women's meetings she was known for being forthright. Her leadership abilities were unquestionable, and she found it easy to deal with all sorts of matters. One of her strengths was said to be her ability to confront and discipline those members that violated policy or practice. Her community spoke highly of her, describing her as helpful and truthful. Her attitude and aptitude were of a prodigious nature.

She was kind and generous. She consistently brewed African beer for the garbage collectors in the area. They would park the garbage truck, go into her yard and enjoy homemade beer. Her children were taught to respect all people, regardless of what work they did. This was a demonstration of the respect and love she had for her community.

Nomahlubi had always wished for a peaceful exit away from this life. She often expressed her disapproval of people around a sick person in hospital. She believed that sick people must not be cluttered by company, but rather they must be given space to recuperate and gather their strength. She suddenly fell very ill one Monday afternoon and had to be taken to hospital. She left her comfortable bed, and had to settle for a hospital bed, upon which she perished and passed on the next day.

#Iknowthisfosho

Even though fear is always lurking around, *NEVER ALLOW IT TO STOP YOU FROM CELEBRATING ALL OF LIFE'S GOODNESS.*

GEORGE KHOSA SECONDARY (GK)

Growing up, school was made up as follows:
- Four years in lower primary, Sub Standard A – Standard 2,
- Four years in higher primary, Standard 3 - 6,
- 3 years in Secondary School, Form 1 – Form 3 and then
- 2 years in High School, Form 4 and Form 5 (Matric)

I could not wait to go to Secondary school. The home I grew up in, is on the main road in one of the townships in Soweto. Daily, I would be envious of the pupils from GK, as we used to call George Khosa Secondary. Beautiful and impeccable in their uniform, they walked past my home from school daily. I knew some, from the church choir and youth guild. I used to look at them with so much envy. In those days there was something prestigious about going to a secondary school and GK, being the only secondary school in our township at the time – nothing beat that.

In January 1974, I was about to start Standard Six, which would be my last year in higher primary. I was counting the months till I could go to GK. One morning, that first week of school, my four class mates and I were called to the principal's office. I was petrified, as I was hardly ever on the wrong side of authority and I wondered what I had done wrong. The principal told us that we were selected to go to GK right away, as the government was experimenting with doing away with standard six. This was going to be an opportunity for the powers that be to observe how we cope and decide if this would work in the future. This opportunity was given to several other pupils in other schools. We could not believe this; we were pleasantly shocked. The principal gave us permission to go home and tell our parents, so we could get back to school the following morning and be taken next door to GK.

I went straight home. My legs could not carry me any faster. My mom was home, so was my aunt who was a school principal in Mpumalanga. Their schools were opening a week later than ours. There was so much joy and excitement at my home. When my father arrived in the evening, he was met with this amazing news. He was so proud of me, his first-born child. The following day we were indeed taken to GK and so my journey in secondary school started, just like that.

We were not well received by the fellow pupils. Their grudge being they were our seniors the year before now we were classmates.

The three years that I spent at GK, were exciting and eventful.

The experience has contributed much in who I have become. I can easily say that my journey into adulthood, started at GK.

I was always serious about life, even though I enjoyed my youth. I was raised by disciplinarians so order and organisation were the order of the day, where I was concerned. Even though I grew up in a religious home, where we attended church on Sundays, it was at GK where I chose to become a Christian, at the SCM. (Student Christian Movement).

Most secondary and high schools had what was known as SCM. This was a non-denominational Christian movement for pupils. It was organised, well-structured and well run. Most schools had a teacher that was responsible for SCM, an overseer. Mr Mashishi was our SCM teacher. We had other teachers who were also Christian, and they served under him. Mr Mashishi was a father to us, not only the SCM pupils but, I would want to believe, all the pupils. He loved God, was a dedicated Christian and leader. Coming to class to teach us, he would sometimes break into a sermonette. I think he got away with this because he was close to retirement and was generally liked by most, if not all.

It was not strange when I was later chosen to become a leader at the SCM. I was raised by a leader - my father. He affirmed us and made us believe and understand that we all are leaders. We got to travel to SCM conferences even out of town. At the time, the school would have normal school trips, sports trips and culture trips. I did not burden my parents with paying for these, as all I wanted to do was travel on SCM trips. The SCM meetings were on Thursdays after school. Mr Mashishi would do the exhortation, the preaching and sometimes he got us student leaders to do that. I started preaching the word at GK. I also started getting invited to preach at other schools around that time.

I was at a wedding recently, and a husband to one of the friends who was also in attendance remarked that I looked familiar. We went through our histories checking where we grew up, went to school, trying to ascertain where we could have met before. After a while, he asked if I never came to their school to preach at their SCM. I could not believe it, he was correct. I cringed because I wondered what I even said in those sermons. That was leadership development from GK.

The late, Mr Mafongosi, my English teacher, was one of my favourites. I loved and enjoyed his class. He made English easy for me. He loved the subject and was passionate. His commitment was to get us to write, understand and speak English properly. I must say he achieved that with most of us.

He did not like the language used in the books by James Hardly Chase, and he made it clear to us all to not read those. He did not want any of us speaking the English as is written in those books. My understanding of his non-approval was that it was not proper English. It was amazing how he could tell if you are a James Hardly Chase reader or not just by listening to how you spoke English and he was hard on those who did.

We did not appreciate him as much at the time, until we left GK for Form Four at other schools. I was amazed when I encountered fellow pupils in high school who struggled with the basics of English, which is when I knew we had a great teacher in Mr Mafongosi.

One of the regrets I have about GK, is the level of corporal punishment we endured from some of the teachers. I literally ran away from the Maths class because I feared the teacher. He induced so much fear in me because of how he used to cane us. He was known as the 30 guy. He gave 30 lashes, as a minimum. Thoughts of it still affect me today. How could it be okay for an adult to give a child 30 lashes? We were in our early teens. So, the fear I had of the teacher cost me, Maths and Physics because they were paired together. I wonder how my career could have gone if I had been able to stay in that subject stream.

We are in a climate now in South Africa, where physical punishment has been abolished both at home and school. I agree that teachers like the 30 lashes teacher, have no place in our democracy, even though discipline is currently a challenge for teachers and parents. Thankfully, most of the teachers that taught us were diligent, and steadfast. GK, remains a highlight in my life.

#Iknowthisfosho

Even with the great changes in the education space, there are new behaviours that inflict fear and cause damage to learners, such as bullying and sexual violence. When parents and other stakeholders remain vigilant and supportive, these behaviours get spotted early enough and also become minimised. ***WE MUST NEVER MINIMISE THE IMPACT OF THESE ON LEARNERS, WE MUST GET THEM COUNSELLED AND SUPPORTED THROUGHOUT.***

16 JUNE 1976

We heard that the pupils at Orlando West High and Morris Isaacson were marching and that there had been trouble with the police, someone heard from the news on radio. We then spotted a friend, who was a pupil at Orlando West High, looking dishevelled. He was in a hurry to get home and we stopped him to ask if the reports were true. He confirmed them and rushed off. It occurred to me much later that he must have been traumatised by what had happened.

There was no turning back after the 16th June 1976. Soweto was on fire, literary and figuratively. There was a policeman, whose home was close to our school. One morning, there was a decision made at my school, to go burn his house. The power and influence of the mob was hair raising. I had a lot of fear, I was scared to participate, and also scared not to. I knew if I didn't, I could get in trouble from the other pupils.

We all went out chanting and something was thrown into the

window and there was a spark: we then all ran away. The police arrested a few pupils, while the rest of us left town. I left with a friend to her relatives, I think in the Vaal area. We were starved of information, there was no way of connecting to hear what was happening. After a few weeks, our parents came to fetch us, and we went back home, back to school. In that period, a lot of school children had been killed, some detained, others left the country.

Around the same time, we had Tsietsi Mashinini and Khotso Seatlholo, the SSRC (Soweto Students Representative Council) Presidents, come to address us at different times. The agenda was very clear: out with the language of the oppressor, Afrikaans, and out with the inferior system of Bantu education.

After both Tsietsi and Khotso fled the country, Trofomo Sono became the SSRC president. I remember one of the things he said when he came to address us. He resisted and was vehemently opposed to the notion that 'half a loaf of bread is better than nothing'. He insisted that we must settle for 'the whole loaf'.

School was never normal from then on. The teachers started fearing the pupils, because all the disciplinary processes were now abandoned. The pupils rejected disciplinary action and became a law unto themselves.

Most of us wanted to complete our academic year. We wrote exams and I passed, and went on to Naledi High School, to do my Form Four. The uprisings continued and I took a break from school and started working.

In 1978, I went back to high school. First year high school, form four, was made up of pupils from different feeder schools. Our high school was new, so we were the first Form 4's and the following year we became the first matriculants, Form 5's. All of us from GK, excelled in our various classes. There was even a rumour spread by one jealous colleague that our high achievement was muti-related.

The school culture changed post 1976. Demonstrations became part of the fabric of schooling. More changes came post 1994, after our first democratic elections in South Africa. Religious education was dropped as a subject in schools. The everyday assembly that included scripture reading and prayers was also dropped. The SCM also fell away.

The authorities did not realise at the time that they were 'throwing the baby out with the bath water'. Pre-democracy, the government schools generally operated from a Christian ethos, except for those communities whose religion was different, like the Muslim communities. There was assembly daily with bible reading and prayers before class. Once a week there was SCM. Post democracy all these were dropped because of the attempt at including other religions.

The authorities did not plan or provide for healthy, impactful alternatives. The vacuum was soon occupied by worse acts of rebellion and practices, such that had never been experienced before. The schools in the townships are the ones more impacted by lawlessness than those in the suburbs. It has become difficult for teachers to instil discipline and rules. There have been numerous attacks, some fatal, on both teachers and pupils by fellow pupils.

Most families from the township take their children to schools in the suburbs, because the schools there are not as impacted as the one's in the township. There are good programmes and projects in the township schools, attempting to bring normality back. There are academic, social and spiritual initiatives.

GK remains one of the many fully operational secondary schools in Dobsonville.

The changes and the impact of June 16, 1976 will stay with us for ever.

#Iknowthisfosho

June 16 1976 brought about gains and losses for us. Gains in terms of the awareness and advancement of the struggle against apartheid and the losses in areas such as school discipline, opening the door to drugs in schools. Parents and teachers need support to move away *FROM FEAR TO ENGAGING* with all the stakeholders to bring normality to schools. *IT IS INVOLVING AND IT IS IMPORTANT TO TURN THINGS AROUND.*

YOUTH ALIVE MINISTRY

Most of us, young people, in the thick of things during the days of apartheid, belonged to youth clubs. I went to Youth Alive Ministry (YAM). The great memories from there still bring a lot of joy to my heart. I know a lot of what I know today, because of YAM. This is a Christian Ministry in Dube, Soweto, which nurtured all of us who were members.

I started going to YAM as a pre-teen right up to when I became a young adult. I then became a parent of YAM going children. I learned about womanhood, leadership, politics, community and diversity. I was also encouraged to study. People that led us, that we looked up to, had gone to school themselves and they continued to impress upon us the importance of education. It is only appropriate to acknowledge the leadership of people like, Bra Mos and Sis Suzan Tsambo, Bra Caesar Molebatsi, Bra Diamond Atong, just to mention a few.

Bra Diamond Atong, what a special man- the man who brought

the late Andrae Crouch to Eyethu cinema in Soweto! My fondest memories of him include watching him problem solve on the spot, dealing with a crisis moment gracefully, even turning it into a fun moment. This one time, he had taken us for a youth camp in the Magalies area, only to arrive there to find that the campsite had either not been booked or there was a double booking. What a crisis, with about 100 young people. Bra Diamond got us all to sit outside, by the gate, He made up a song to keep us busy, and we were happy to participate. We sang, 'I want to eat eight apples and bananas. We used all five vowels with every verse, and it was the funniest thing ever. We sang:

'E wente et, e wente et, et epples end benenes
I winti it, I wint it, it ipplis ind bininis
O wonto ot, ownto ot, ot opplos ond bononos
U wuntu ut, uwuntu u, ut upplus und bununus'

We had a lot of fun with this, and we were not perturbed by the problem. We just knew a plan will come up. The joys of being young and carefree. It did. We ended up in that campsite for all the days we had contracted for.

We went to camp every end of the year and as a leader, we were part of the planning. I have led and served in various areas at YAM. I cooked at camp, I looked after sick people, I was a cabin leader, I counselled others, I oversaw the programme. One of the most memorable camps was when we went to Durban. Most of the young people had never been to the sea side before so there was a lot of anticipation and excitement. One of our leaders, Bra Edgar Mehlomakhulu, used to bring about so much excitement when he spoke about Durban. The trip was going to be by train, he told us that we would know we were entering Durban when we could touch and pluck bananas just by extending our hands outside of the windows. The leadership team went ahead of the entire group and we drove, so we missed out on the train experience.

Discipline at YAM, was uncompromising. There was a code of conduct when we travelled and if anyone disobeyed, they would be sent back home. Parents knew that the environment was not fertile to disorder or lawlessness. I remember one young woman being sent home because she snuck her boyfriend into her room – the boyfriend had 'visited' all the way from Soweto. This was not allowed.

There was a time when the youth meetings in Dube took place on Friday evenings. My parents refused for my brother and I to attend because they felt it was risky to be out at that time of the evening, even though there was transport to bring us back home safely. It was always risky letting young people out on their own at night. Parents were rightfully fearful. Bra Diamond came to my house to negotiate and assure my parents that it was all well. My brother and I were anxious about what the outcome of the meeting was going to be. In a short space of time he had my parents in his hand, they were all laughing and comfortable with each other, and we were given permission to attend.

Bra Mandla Adonisi was another leader that we had at YAM. He taught me how to run meetings and how to lead. You could never attend his meetings unprepared. He had no tolerance for mediocrity of any kind. Once in a meeting, a fellow youth leader was responding to a question and he started, in an apologetic way, by saying, he is not sure but...'   Bra Mandla viciously, stopped him right there, and told him that if he was not sure, he ought to be quiet. Attending Bra Mandla's meetings brought about some anxieties especially if you were not delivering on agreed upon goals.

Bra Mandla started studying at UNISA, at the time when he was our leader at YAM. He carried on until he graduated with a PHD degree. By the time he died, in 2017, he was a well-respected in his field and was a senior lecturer at GIBS. This was a man who was articulate, forthright and a man of his word. A great model to us growing up, even when we had become adults.

Bishop Mosa Sono's tribute at Bra Mandla's funeral was beautiful and befitting. The bishop spoke about his experience of becoming born again at YAM. As all this was new to him, he had a visit from Bra Mandla, who went on to disciple him in his early stages of becoming a born again Christian. In those days, discipleship was done by regular meetings, to go through the scriptures and to explain the process to new converts.

YAM was a beautiful, safe, dynamic environment. The debates and discussions, were always on a different level. There were times when the discussions went above my head- when theologians, activists and academics used to visit. I am very happy for YAM, to have been part of my life. There are a lot of other leaders at YAM that I continue to respect. Some of the friendships from then, still exist in my life today.

#Iknowthisfosho

My life is **RICHER** because I saw my parents **FACE THEIR FEARS** by letting us go out to YAM at night.

We are better off **FACING OUR FEARS** than running from them.

YOUTH AWARENESS CLUB

My brother asked me to come join a panel of speakers at their youth club. They were having a panel discussion on the role of youth in the then environment of political struggle and everything that went with it. He said they needed someone to speak on religion as all the other aspects had speakers and this one had no takers. I was overwhelmed and excited, a response that for a long time has characterised my response to life; a combination of being overwhelmed and excited.

I did not really know the other panellists, except for a few of his friends, who were members of this youth club. My belief then was that everybody else was smarter than I was. I agreed; I felt like I had no other option. He believed that I could do it and for a moment that was good enough for me.

Something happens to one's body in moments where there is no congruency. Even when the mouth says yes, the body always tells its own truth. I was afraid that the truth from my body, would be more visible to the audience than what I would say.

The day came and even though I had prepared, I was in panic mode. My brother was smart, articulate and opinionated and could hold down an argument. I felt that I was perhaps expected to be like him, smart and great at presenting arguments. There were five speakers. I was the fourth, the only woman and outsider. In trying to listen to the other speakers before me, the voice in my head, as usual, kept telling me how I did not measure up, how they all were very articulate and smart and how I did not make the cut.

I suddenly had to talk myself out of what was going on in my head. I realised the power of having already showed up, so I was not about to compromise on being fully present. I would give it my best.

My turn came. I stood up, looked at the audience and shared a bit about myself. I faked confidence, all the way as I went through my presentation. I benefited greatly from my preparation, and I already knew about the breathing technique, so I used it. Then it was time for questions and comments and my heart was pounding. I suddenly felt a slight headache. I truly thought they were now going to find out that I was not as gifted as my brother. They were generous with their comments and appreciated my input to the subject. I left feeling 'safe' and still not convinced that I had added value to the discussion. The voice in my head kept telling me the reason they were soft on me was because they did not know me well enough and also they respected by brother.

I have often felt this way about myself. Plagued by self-doubt and in fear of being exposed as a fraud. My parents and brother were confident and assertive, yet I wasn't. I used then to measure myself against them and I came very short. My brother was very impressed and full of praise at my presentation.

Interestingly, I became a member at this youth club. The members were smart, highly intellectual so were the leaders. The conversations and activities really stretched and steered us towards growth, something I have always appreciated. I was eventually able to own the fact that I could hold my own in the space. I participated in conversations, had relevant input to share. There was always an interest from others to know what I thought on matters. I also argued my points whenever I was challenged. I started to gain confidence in myself and in my ideas.

Much later in my life, sadly after she already passed, I began to truly appreciate my mother's strength of character. I began to draw from my knowledge of her. I allowed myself to entertain thoughts of how she would respond, if she were in my situation, at a given time. I think this helped me develop a positive sense of self even further.

Coming from a highly politicised family and era, I was surrounded by political geniuses, most of whom I knew through my brothers. Some were friends from school and university. I however never really belonged to a particular movement. My family belonged to the Black Consciousness Movement of Azania. I was never able to shrug off the identity of Black Consciousness earlier, now I fully embrace it, even though my expression thereof is not within an organisation.

#Iknowthisfosho

Our bodies speak: sometimes louder than our mouths. It is therefore important to check for alignment *BETWEEN WHAT WE SAY AND WHAT OUR BODIES SAY.*

Sometimes the gracious thing to do is to *OWN UP TO FEAR*, in whatever way it manifests, so that we can remain authentic.

FEAR – UPBRINGING

I grew up fearful. I am the eldest child to my parents, who were loving and committed in their role of parenting. I always knew that they wanted the best for me, for us. My mother was very strict and also forthright. She spoke her mind with power.
I was intimidated by her power, growing up. I did not like her forthrightness and I purposed to not be like that. Only as I grew older did I start to appreciate her audacity, how she stood up for what she believed, how she got stuff done, her presence and how she commanded respect.

I sometimes felt like my non-assertiveness at the time, was a disappointment to her. I doubted myself a lot. I knew I was loved but it felt like she expected more from me than I could offer. I could never articulate that in a conversation and as a result, there were issues I could never raise with my mother. Even though we were physically punished by both our parents, we never felt less loved, we felt affirmed as children growing up.

Steve Biko spoke about fear, how fear, as a result of oppression, has robbed us as black people. He warned us to rather fear, fear itself. It resonates with what I know and what I have been taught, having been raised by fearless parents. I, however, have had to unlearn the fear that had previously paralysed me and resulted in my lack of action. I love the fact that the bible also carries the same message of not being fearful. It is often said that, most of the things we worry about, things we are fearful of, never happen, and so fear is largely, a waste of emotions.

I have seen fear in action. In bullying, in controlling, in addiction and in many other areas of life. In re-reading some of Robert Kiyosaki's works, he articulates how negative it is to have fear as a motivator. He mentions that as an entrepreneur, success is almost impossible, when one operates from fear. Fear makes us crave security, and entrepreneurship does not provide security, he attests.

What you need instead is faith, as an entrepreneur. After you have researched and done all your market analysis, you boldly step out to do your thing, believing that you will be successful.

As an entrepreneur, you need courage as described by Nelson Mandela: *'I learned that courage was not the absence of fear, but the triumph over it. The brave man is not he who does not feel afraid, but he who conquers that fear.'*

Fear destroys dreams before they are realised, ideas that are waiting to be birthed are aborted out of fear. Fear breeds the attitude of hoarding, believing that there isn't enough for all of us. Fear is responsible for keeping most people stuck where they are, in dysfunctional relationships and jobs. Fear makes people scared to laugh and express their love for life.

Freedom from the fear of fear, remains my aspiration.

#Iknowthisfosho

The thing to be
feared, is fear itself
FAITH IS NOT POSSIBLE
WHERE FEAR REIGNS.

FREE FROM FEAR!

My love for swimming was birthed very early, in my teens. I learnt how to swim at our local swimming pool in Dobsonville. The municipality employed an instructor who also was a life saver.

This came in handy whenever I went on youth camps because we had access to swimming pools. We did not, at the time, anticipate that we would have swimming pools in our homes, so again this was a huge benefit.

My first time at the University of the Witwatersrand, I was struck by the size and positioning of the pool there. I had never before swum in such a big pool. How I wish I could. Every day I had a desire to swim in that pool. Yet, my mind asked "How could I?". I did not have the right   type body to go swim there. I was overweight and very self-conscious of my imperfect body. I noticed how almost all the girls at the pool where slim with "perfect bodies". Every time I walked past the pool, which was almost every day, I envied the girls by the pool, I was jealous of

them having what I thought to be perfect bodies and me being overweight, how could life be so unfair, I thought?
I could not shake off the feeling of wanting to get inside the pool, even with all the unpleasant things that used to be said about overweight people. I used to imagine myself inside the water, enjoying the pool and being comfortable. Whenever those mental pictures came, the voice in my head would be loud to discredit me, as a result I remained outside the pool, safe from all the possible criticism.

One day, I looked at the pool and at the people by the pool and I thought to myself, "What is the worst thing that could happen if I go inside the pool?". That is apart from all the water being splashed out of the pool when an overweight person gets in, as the myth went. The worst thing could be people laughing and ridiculing me. So, I though, laughter and ridicule I can stand. I got myself ready for possible laughter and ridicule. Suddenly, my eyes opened, I had a moment of courage and wisdom descending on me. I felt lighter, I decided to go swim, and it felt right.

As I headed for the change room, my heart was pounding, I felt hot and cold like a pre-menopausal woman. It felt like my entire life depended on this move. My thighs and legs wobbled like jelly. As I took one step after the other, I kept hearing the voice in my head, telling me to go back. It felt like a do or die moment. I looked up at the amphitheatre and I was confused by what I thought was the mood and temperament of the people sitting there.

I continued to look around as I went into the changing room

to change. I was hoping for some approval, some affirmation. There was none. Everyone got about their business. I got out of the change room and I felt like all the eyes were on me. It felt like people looking were wondering what I was about to do. I moved down to the pool, and as I got closer, I was amazed. I suddenly noticed how everyone was minding their own business. I got inside the pool and I felt well received. I wondered why I waited for so long. I had just tasted and experienced freedom. I felt free indeed. Freedom from the fear of judgement. Freedom from the opinions of others, free to be me. My life was never the same after that.

That became the first of many times that I swam in that pool. Something big had shifted. My friends and colleagues celebrated my courage. They did not know what it took for me to take that step. Some disclosed later, that they also had harboured a fear of exposing their imperfect bodies. I did not know at the time that going into that pool, freed, not only me, but a few others who would not have dared. My fear of what people would say was gone. I gradually got into a place where I did not rush into the pool after taking off my sarong or towel, big body and all. I was free, I am free. The fear was broken, what an achievement.

I have embraced this approach in my work as well. I have learned to treat my inner voice not as an authority but more as any voice giving me suggestions. The answer from me is sometimes a yes and sometimes a no. There is no voice that I allow to dominate me, to send me back to fear. Of course, fear has not stopped from trying to have permanent residence, in my head. I take every day as an opportunity to live fearlessly.

In the same way that I saw myself walk into the pool and swim despite my initial fears. I allow myself to bravely walk into spaces and places I could easily have disqualified myself from because of my body size, my history or anything that I feel makes me inadequate.

I am enough and able.

#Iknowthisfosho

The voices in your head can be silenced:
jump into the pool and see them go silent.
There are many people waiting to be set
free from fear, by you conquering your own
'swimming pool'.

INTENTIONALITY–
PASSING MATRIC

My matric results came out when I was away at the Youth Alive Ministries camp. Going to youth camp every end of the year was my usual routine.

The leaders kept all of us away from the news back at home, including the matric results. Thankfully there was no social media then. We really were not concerned and were at peace with waiting until we got home to find out about our results. We were a big group and it would be unpleasant to find out away from family, because there would always be those who didn't make it.

I remember coming back from camp and seeing my two uncles' cars parked outside. As I got closer, no one could hide their smiles. They told me I had passed with exemption, university entrance, and there was great excitement. My uncles were special to me. I had four. Three lived in Soweto, one in Mpumalanga. One of them, had a penchant for speed, my mom used to call him a 'two minutes to Joburg' kind of driver. Whenever he bought a new car, he would come to show my mom and I would go with him for a drive instead. I think I was his favourite niece, we got on beautifully. It was always a joyous moment whenever any of my uncles visited, the local ones visited a lot.

Not so long after that, it was time to go to university. I went to Fort Hare University, with some of my friends. Fort Hare University then, was known as a black university. Some of our prestigious leaders on the continent studied at Fort Hare, like Nelson Mandela, Robert Mugabe. It is known for its rich history.

I must be honest, there wasn't much thought to the decision of where and what to study. I had not been admitted as yet, I don't even remember if I had applied. Those days we could safely do self-applications, there was always accommodation. Unfortunately, a late application might mean the course that one wants to embark on is fully subscribed, as was my case. I was not going to come back home, so I looked for a course where there was accommodation. I then settled for a degree in teaching. Not that I had ever wanted to be a teacher.

The year was riddled with demonstrations, and all sorts of political upheavals as was the tone and theme in the entire country. I failed at the end of the year. I was distraught, it was my first time failing ever! My school experience had been excellent. I got high marks continuously, I expected the same at university. I had to become honest with myself. I did not set an intention. I was happy to just flow with everything and everyone, and my results could attest to that.

We went back at the beginning of the following year and I managed to register for social work, which is what I had wanted to do from the onset. Halfway through the year, with the political situation having continued to be volatile, most of us we were dismissed for participating in demonstrations, my Fort Hare university experience ended abruptly.

I found work a few months later and my plan was to save money so I could go back to university. I passed on opportunities that could make it difficult for me to go back to university full time, like buying a home and a car, as I had a clear intention of studying full time. It took me eight years, to finally go back, full time. I resigned and registered at the University of the Witwatersrand, for Social work. At that stage, my intention was clear. I was going for a BA Social Work Honours.

I already was a mother to my son, who must have been around 2 years of age at the time. My folks had kindly agreed to look after him, whilst I studied. The psychological struggle was intense. I had a relatively good, secured job. My colleagues thought I was crazy. Why resign, when I could study part time, they enquired. There were moments, where I doubted my decision, wondering to myself, 'what if they are right?'

That doubt and fear crept in again, I sometimes had thoughts that I might not even make it. I would sometimes think, my job is okay, it is secured and maybe I should just stay. At times, I felt like my colleagues were daring me. What was going to happen if I failed? I would have lost my good job with nothing to show for it. I would be embarrassed to face them, thinking they would mock me. The drive to go study was more intense. I thought I had everything inside to enable me to make it. I had made up my mind, I was doing it!

I silenced the inner voices and immersed myself in my studies. The stakes were too high. There was no way I could allow myself to fail. I was a full-time student at residence, an opportunity I am grateful for. Life in residence was exciting. It is very easy to just get lost in all of it. I did not have that luxury; I was vigilant because I was on a mission. I remember how I would sometimes turn down offers to go out. I was committed to pass. One time, a friend invited me on a night out with other friends. I declined, I had work to do for the next day. I still remember her response, she said to me, "So what if you submit late, no one is going to punish you". I still did not go out with them that night.

My intention was set, very clear. At the end of four years I completed my BA Social Work Honours, and I graduated. It was a big moment for me. My big lesson was the power on possibility, the power of intention. I started very decisively and intentionally. I passed my degree in record time.

SETTING AN INTENTION,
is crucial. It is the first step to
achieving one's goals.

———————————————

INTENTIONALITY 2 – MY NAME

I was named Patricia Lesiah Motlalepule, those are names in all my formal documents. When I started school, I was registered as Lecia. During the apartheid era, most of us had to have English names for school and church and then our African language names for when we were at home with family and friends. Strangely, I was called Lecia, almost everywhere, except by my family and relatives. I envied the children who did not have English names. They were few. I could not relate neither could I fathom, the resistance from their parents, in not giving them English names.

The advent of the BCM, (the Black Consciousness Movement of Azania) brought with it the culture of black pride. We started loving our hair, our dark skins and our African names. I remember making an announcement to whoever was there listening, that from that day on, I would no longer respond to being called Lecia, I would go by my Setswana name Motlalepule.

I was told this was going to be a problem because white people are not going to be able to say Motlalepule. I cannot even remember my response, I could not be bothered, change had come. It took a while for the people around me to get used to the new name, I was patient and deliberate in reminding them, every time they 'forgot' and called me Lecia.

I remember once my father calling me at work. I answered the phone and he asked to speak with Lecia. I was gobsmacked. My dad, he was old school like that, a generation that was brutalised by apartheid. He did not know any better. I told him on the phone, that my name, is Motlalepule.

He asked about the white people. Everyone worried about the white people. During apartheid, we had to worry about how white people would respond to what we said, what we did, how we showed up. If they decided it was offensive, they could get one arrested. I hated that; I still do.

African people, especially Batswana, know that Motlalepule is sometimes shortened to Tlale, or Puli, or Mpule. The shortened version that somehow just took off is Tlale. I do not introduce myself as Tlale often, though. I always like people, especially the non- Setswana speakers to familiarise themselves with Motlalepule, before they can call me Tlale. The trick is by the time they master saying Motlalepule, it is too much trouble to now learn calling me Tlale.

My late mother, being an Um-Xhosa, had given me an isiXhosa name. She called me Nqhose. My late aunt, some of my cousins and one neighbour also called me Nqhose. Those are the only people who use the name Nqhose. Once, some white people were complaining that they struggle to say Motlalepule, they asked if I don't have another name, hoping for an English name. I told them my other name was Nqhose, they asked me to rather help them learn to say Motlalepule.

I feel a connection when someone calls me by name, the name I have chosen. Apartheid gave white people a right to impose English or Afrikaans names on us. When a white person addressed me as Patricia or Lecia, I could not argue.

It was fearful to go against a white person because this would land one in trouble. I did not want trouble, I avoid trouble. Being white meant being right all the time and being black meant the direct opposite. The sense and extent of demoralisation at this experience can only be understood by having experienced it.

Our political past was not kind to our identity, to our African names. Apartheid brutalised us black people in every way possible. Our culture was made out as inferior; our names were said to not be Christian. God was made out as white; hence Christian names could only be white.

Embracing my African name, and insisting of using it, was part of my emancipation, of owning my heritage and of saying to myself, I matter, as an African. Choosing to be called Motlalepule, was my own campaign against having to respond to a name that was meaningless to me. I exercised my power of choice, something that did not exist during apartheid. Apartheid was embedded in fear. I am free

Today, I react whenever I'm called Patricia or Lecia. Those names to me, represent oppression, represent apartheid. I become emotional when I meet people in offices or institutions who want to insist on using those names in addressing me. White dominance is still a reality in SA.

I am Motlalepule Mokhine.

#Iknowthisfosho

I DON'T NEED PERMISSION
to celebrate my name.
All our names are beautiful.

———————————

RECIPROCITY

Reciprocity can be tricky. It is probably normal to expect those we love and heap with gifts and support to do the same for us. Sometimes they do. My belief is that we are called to bless those who are not necessarily positioned to bless us at the time.

When you operate from reciprocity, you are forced to keep count of who did what to you and for you and who didn't. 'She did not greet me back, am not greeting her next time'

'She did not support me when I was going through challenges, am not going all out for her either'.

You count and keep score of what is done to you so you can give back in equal measure. It can be exhausting.

Think about God for a moment. Think how many times you messed up and He kept on loving you. Think how He never took away His blessings on your life. Think how you are standing;

despite all you have gone through.

Isn't life about paying it forward? In my experience, I don't get to directly bless the people who have blessed me. I appreciate opportunities to be a blessing to others, often, it is not the same people who have been a blessing towards me. I do think that is how we ought to live. It also is short-sighted to now wait for the people you have done favours for, to do favours for you.

It is pleasing to give, to open doors for others when you can. It is true that in life we reap what we sow. The amazing thing with social media now is the ability to give directly to strangers. This reminds us how heart-warming it can be to contribute to a cause where no one will ever know that you did.

Giving to others is also about the mindset. When you approach life with an abundance frame of mind, you can give freely without keeping count or expecting anything in return. The scarcity mentality is costly: it robs one from experiencing the joy of giving. It pulls one to an attitude of hoarding due to a fear of not having enough. I have always believed that there is enough for all of us.

Emulate God, love people, even those who do not love you back. There are people who already love you. Give as the scripture says, *freely you have received, freely give.* Stop counting.

#Iknowthisfosho

There is enough in
this world **FOR ALL OF US.**

THE FEAR OF DOWNGRADING: KEEPING UP WITH THE BUTHELEZI'S?

Downgrading is tough, especially if it is not voluntary. It invokes feelings of shame, failure and defeat. We live in times in which we are more respected because of what those around us think we have, materially. Once our ability to move up or maintain those levels, is threatened, trouble brews.

I earned my first pay cheque as a nurse and as expected this was a very exciting moment. I joined my friends on my first pay day, and we hit the shops. I bought shoes and other clothing items and could not wait to get home to show my folks. I should have known better. My father was upset as I unpacked and showed him my new shoes. "Don't you have shoes?' he asked, I wondered what was wrong with him.

My father lectured us about everything. Savings, healthy living, being aware of your surrounding for your own security, and more. As I had started working, my father was waiting for me to show him my savings plan. I was in my late teens, and all I wanted was freedom to spend.

Years later, I'd been to university, changed careers and acquired my first home – a townhouse in a brand-new complex. With the excitement of working and wanting it all, I got myself in financial trouble. I was overspending on credit cards and overdrafts, as well as store cards. I reached a stage where I was so overwhelmed, I was becoming depressed. I had thoughts and images of losing it all and becoming blacklisted. I did not follow what my father had taught me. A friend suggested I speak to someone who could help.

I spoke to him and this opened my eyes. I had to face my reality and make tough decisions. I could not cope. I had to downgrade. It was painful. I thought about the perceptions that existed about me, perceptions of being organised and professional: from having my own home, to not affording it: how these perceptions were being shattered through this experience. Fear of being seen as a failure gripped me. I was anxious of how my relationships would be affected by this.

Fortunately, both my parents were still alive, and were financially stable. They allowed me to live with them and I rented my house out. I used the rent money to service the bond and my folks allowed me space to pay off what I needed to and did not pressure me to contribute much in their house. One of my friends thought I was brave to do that. She told me she could never downgrade her standard of living, no matter what. I truly felt blessed being at my parents, sorting myself out financially.

If I did not have parents that were resourceful and willing to assist, it would have taken me a long time to recover. I learned my lesson. After a few months. I was back on my feet and I moved out to be on my own, again. I was wiser and I try to live within my means. I have learned to go without stuff that I cannot afford, difficult yes, but do-able.

Most people I know have had a moment where they considered downgrading their standard of living. Very few go ahead and do it. The reality is downgrading comes at an emotional cost. You are judged negatively; I know better now that judgement from others could never make me lose sleep. I love good and beautiful things. I also am protective of my heart, my peace.

The reality is most people do get to a stage in their lives where things are becoming unbearable and if they are truthful and honest, they know they need to downgrade.

I think a good place to be in life is where one's identity is not linked to stuff.

A couple that I know, fell on hard times in recent years. They both lost their jobs around the same time. Things became much tougher financially, and they could not afford private school for their children anymore, they kept the children at home, instead of taking them to a public school. It was too embarrassing and humiliating for them to downgrade. I was touched by the cost of the fear they endured. Their children suffered because they could not face being humiliated by their friends and colleagues. Fear is costly.

Yet in the same breath, I met a couple that continues to inspire me. He is a middle-income earner and the wife is a stay at home mum home schooling their children. They live in a modest house in the suburbs. He has been driving the same car he drove when I met them the first time, over 10 year ago, at the time of writing. He has looked after this car and it is serving him very well. The reality though is he pays no car instalment. Their life is very simple. I have learned and experienced gratitude in a big way from this family. Their focus is on providing for their children, educating them and giving them rich life experiences that are valuable – not necessarily full of 'stuff".

It takes a particular type of mindset to willingly downgrade. It is about giving oneself permission to re-group, to start all over again and be restored. This is a valley experience that is rich with lessons. I don't know people who did not come out wiser from a downgrading experience.

The fear of resisting a necessary downgrade is very costly.

#Iknowthisfosho

Stuff should never define who you are. Find meaning in your relationships and in your contribution to the lives of others.

There is always someone who looks at you and wishes they had what you have: let that sink in.

———————————————

MEN IN OUR SOCIETY

I would like like to pay tribute to the good men in our lives. In a world riddled with rampant abuse of women by men, it is important to appreciate men who are great citizens, who are responsible, who get on with what they are called to do. We see you.

I want to honour and salute these men. They are good husbands, partners and fathers to their families. They are by no means perfect; they are very committed to giving their best.

Some of them don't necessarily have access to a lot of money or connections, yet they make sure their families are well taken care of.

One can hear the criticism and disgust in some women who've been left alone to take care of children, a child whose father left when she was a baby or toddler or the focus on some fathers who are at home and yet do not provide for their family out of choice. I live in this society; I know those things exist.

What makes a good man? The role of men has come under fire in our times because of their perceived roles, the experience many women have had. Some of these include but are not limited to:

- The fact that it is men who rape and abuse women and children
- Some men neglect and leave women to take care of their children
- Some of them kill their partners and children when they cannot cope or are overwhelmed with jealousy.
- Others get involved in illegal activities and end up in jail leaving women to look after the rest of the families.
- Some travel and work away from home, missing out on the experience of their children's development and there are consequences for that.

All these have contributed to having men branded as horrible and not caring. I salute all those men who are present, within their families, who despite the economic situation have remained committed in their role as providers and protectors.

I salute those who have stayed committed to their role as comforters, nurturers and counsellors in their homes – who make time to listen to their partners and children, who encourage and attend sports activities even if their child is a reserve in the team. The man who is interested in the development of their partner, who will help her enhance her career.

I salute the men who will sacrifice going out with his friends occasionally to spend time playing and entertaining their children in the park or watching videos at home with them.

I salute men who are concerned when their partners are not happy, when they feel embarrassed or humiliated, when they feel down, and these types of men remain present.
A man who doesn't let the lack of money or other resources stand in the way of being supportive to his children and partner is a blessing.

I salute men who organise to get boys taught to be great men in the future, men who are role models for these boys and for other men.
My wish is that the men in communities can strive to be good fathers, partners and community members. As a woman, I am pleased when we support each other in families and create an environment that will facilitate caring, love and good things to emerge.

I salute men who don't justify women abuse.

I salute men who do not abuse their partners and other women around them.

Philippians 4:8 – *"Finally, brethren, whatever things are true, whatever things are noble, whatever things are just, whatever things are pure, whatever things are of good report, if there is any virtue and if there is anything praiseworthy – meditate on these things."*

#Iknowthisfosho

Becoming fearless **IS NOT INHERITED**, it's a journey to be **ENDURED AND ARRIVED AT ON MY OWN.**

MY BELOVED HOME, GROWING UP

Winter mornings were the best. The ones where you hear the wind howl and whistle whilst you are nicely cuddled in your warm bed. My mother used to get up early to make fire in her Jewel stove. She would not allow us to get out of bed until the kitchen was warm enough. She would pull up a bench by the fire for me and my two brothers to sit, enjoying the fire. She would make us tea and bread and then prepare water for us to be washed before we set off for school.

As the eldest, my parents spoiled me. It took my parents a while to have children, to have me. They so much wanted to start a family, and nothing was happening. My mother was under a lot of pressure, as a new makoti (bride). Then one day, they conceived, and I was born. I am told there was a big party, to celebrate my birth, a cow was slaughtered, a whole cow! My mother liked to celebrate, of course celebrating my birth was relevant. I am grateful for the love I have enjoyed from my parents. My dad taught me that I am great, I am beautiful, I am enough. My mom indulged me in all girly things. My parents though were strict. I hated how strict they were then, now I am pleased they were. Aside from SCM (Students Christian Movement) and later YAM (Youth Alive Ministries), we were not allowed out, as children. Only one Sunday afternoon a month, I was allowed out. I thought they were mean. This feeling was only because the rest of my friends could go out whenever they wanted to.

I got most of the things I wanted as a child. I was not a demanding child, so I never asked for impossible things. My home was full of love and that was enough. I knew my parents wanted the best for me. What also helped was the fact that my mother was a hard worker, a workaholic of sorts. My mum could spoil my Saturday by deciding, in the morning, that it was a day for spring cleaning. As a child, I was never expected to have plans. So, when mom decided, it was settled- spring cleaning it was.

We had a tradition in the township, of dressing up on Christmas day and/or New Year's Day. I remember how I was almost always one of the best dressed because my mother outsourced this shopping to a family friend, ausi Thapelo Mzizi and she was too brilliant at this.

When I was in secondary school, my father was in what is now known as the School Governing Body (SGB), they were called School Committees then and did not have the power the current SGB's have. One Saturday morning, one of my teachers came to my house to chat to my father about the school committee matters. My mom was up, sweeping and preparing breakfast while the kitchen was getting warm. The teacher asked my father about my whereabouts and he told the teacher I was in bed still.

My father had no idea how compromising that would be for me. The teacher's idea of a child's role was never to be negotiated. Her mind was made. I could just imagine how mad she was to hear that I was in bed still.

Monday came, the dreaded Monday. The teacher stormed into class. The expression on her face was telling, left nothing to the imagination. I knew what was coming. She addressed me. *'Mokhine, stand up, a ke le mmoneng! Mmabotswa! Mmage o fiela lebala, a robetse yena. Mozalwane!'* ("Mokhine, get up, just look at her! She's so lazy! Her mother is sweeping the yard while she is sleeping. And she calls herself a Christian"). I was never given an opportunity to respond, that's how things were in those days, and I never heard the end of that story.

My redemption was that I continuously did well in class and in her subjects. She was great at teaching and we admired the fact she had a university degree, she was the only teacher with a university degree, and she would openly brag about that. I admired her poise, she walked with so much confidence that I wanted to be like her when I grew up.

The one thing we did not appreciate was her attitude to some pupils. She was derogatory and if your performance was not great, she would humiliate you. In those days, mental health was not a big thing to worry about. I can only imagine, how many had their sense of worth negatively impacted by her.

Thankfully, by the time the teacher passed on, I was an adult already, and we were on good terms. She had become converted and became a staunch Christian, which was beautiful to watch, after she had criticised me of being one myself.

Another negative experience at primary was a class teacher who thought she was being adult and disciplining us, but her actions scarred the pupils she tried to admonish. A girl in my class was 18 years old and just starting school, this was not unique as she was from the rural areas. There had been instances where fathers would resist sending their daughters to school. This girl started dating and news soon spread that she had a boyfriend. The teacher confronted her and openly humiliated her in front of the entire class. She ended up dropping out of school. We did not have counsellors at school that could have supported her in that time. That is just how things were, in those days.

I survived all these teachers because my parents went out of their way to make me feel worthy.

#Iknowthisfosho

Nothing beats the love and sense of security a child gets from home, it serves as a foundation against all other voices they encounter.

You **DON'T NEED WEALTH TO CREATE A LOVING ENVIRONMENT** for your family, as well as to raise well-adjusted children. *YOU NEED A HEART FULL OF FEARLESSNESS, LOVE, AND FORGIVENESS.*

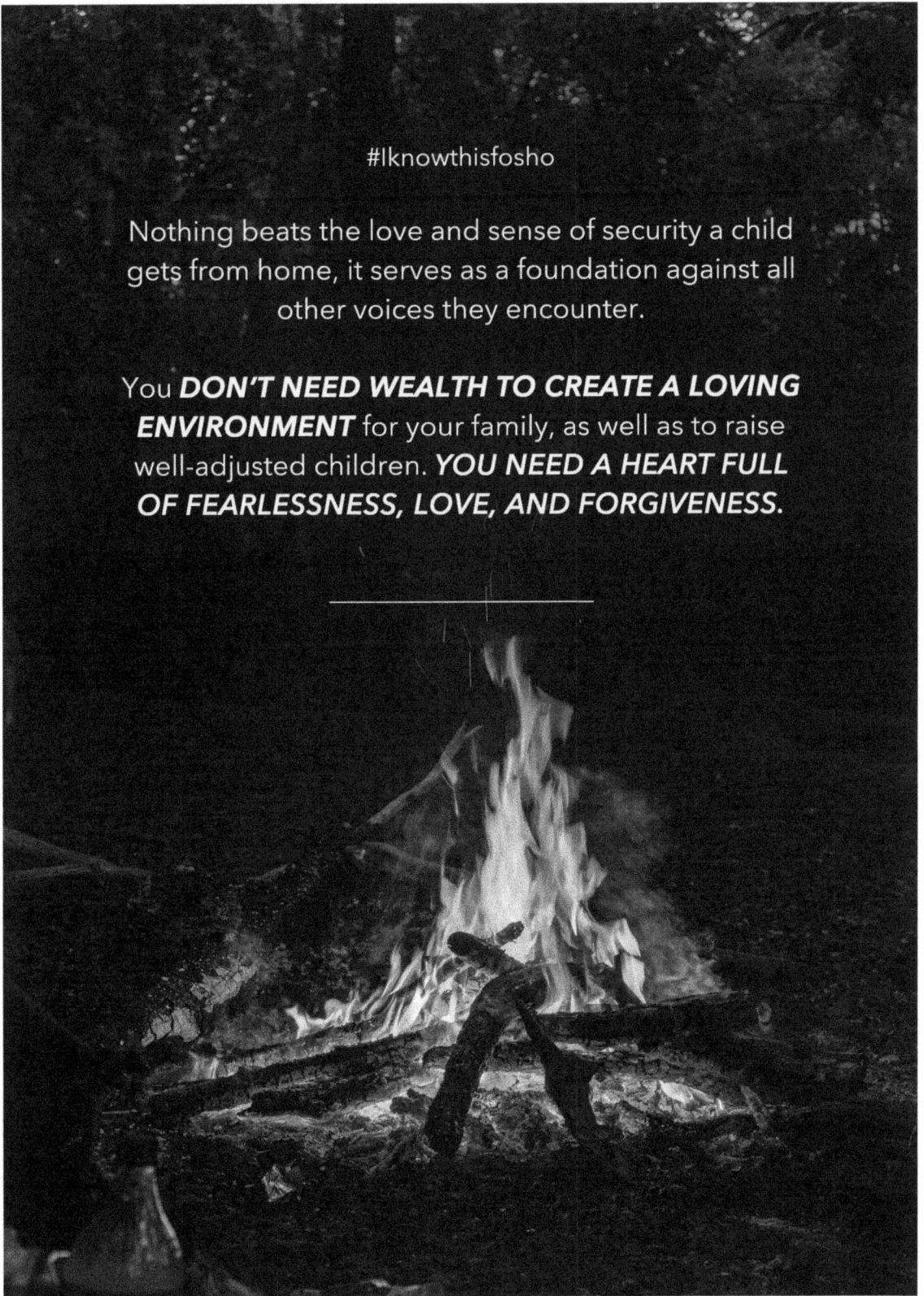

MY GOOD SAMARITAN

There was a time in my teens when I wanted to go to boarding school. Boarding school seemed cooler and I was not impressed that my parents did not even want to have that conversation. The girls who attended boarding schools looked superior, like they came from rich families because they wore the best of clothes and accessories. They would walk up and down the street, with co-ordinated outfits, hair proper and fashionable, oozing confidence. I also wanted that.

One day, before school resumed in January, I decided to go to Mafikeng (now Mahikeng) without my parent's knowledge and permission, to apply at a boarding school. I was naïve and innocent. I didn't even consider whether my parents could afford a boarding school or not. Besides they were too protective, I believe the reason I didn't discuss this decision was because I avoided attempts for them to get me to abandon the plan. I trusted my instincts and my decision, and it felt so right. So, I set out to find myself a boarding school.

I left in the morning, by taxi and it's a long trip from Soweto. By the time I was done, disappointed at having not secured a place, I realised that I could not get back home timeously and safe. I knew no one in the area, I was in a township called Montshiwa - not even sure how I got there. The sensible thing was to stay the night and travel back in the morning.

I randomly just went into one house, and found a man, a father figure. I am amazed at how non-threatening all this was for me. I assumed the wife and children would be coming in later. I told him my story and he said I could stay. The amazing thing about those days is that crime was low, all older people were parents to all the children. They could rebuke any child, set them on the right path, irrespective of whether they had a relationship with the parents or not. Older people were generally protectors of younger people.

This man gave me food, offered me a bath and a bedroom and at around 7pm, he went to bed in the other room. Thankfully, I did not expect anything different. I looked at this man, same way I looked at my father. A father figure, who was there to protect and look after children.

So, I slept peacefully. In the morning, he offered me breakfast, told me he was leaving for work. He left me in his house, told me what to do when I leave. I was to lock the house, and he had told me where to leave the keys. I did exactly that.

He never told me his name, did not ask for my name, nothing. When I think about this encounter now, I get shivers down my spine. This is one of the "good old times" encounters, that one wishes could make a comeback. What an amazing encounter with a stranger who treated me like family. There are good people out there who will support, with no expectations and with no ulterior motives.

#Iknowthisfosho

IN A WORLD THAT HAS BECOME CRUEL AND UNSAFE, YOU CAN CHOOSE TO BE THE KIND ONE.WE ARE SURROUNDED BY MANY KIND PEOPLE, WHO DO NOT WANT ANYTHING IN RETURN FOR THEIR KINDNESS. RECEIVE KINDNESS.

_____

WHAT EXPOSURE?

'Starting out in business is NOT always easy. Not only did I have to use my personal funds to get set up I also had to get my name out there while making sure that I grew my business.

One of the first hurdles to cross was the numerous companies that were happy to give me "exposure" and not pay me. I did have an expectation of being paid, for work I did, which is normal.

I found myself trying to strike the right balance, as a new player I definitely could do with exposure. Early on I remember dealing with a TV station that had a daily 5-minute motivation slot and used various people to share and motivate its viewers. An acquaintance of mine who worked there recommended my services. I was asked to come record 10 slots that would be broadcast over a two-week period. My excitement was short-lived as I soon learned that I wouldn't be paid as they used this slot to give exposure to the speakers. I prepared for 10 episodes of five minutes each. On the day of recording, I went armed with a suitcase full of 10 different outfits and we had an all-day recording session.

While one may initially look at this and immediately think it was not worth it, I thought to make the best of the opportunity and ask for the final recordings so that I may also use them in the future. While this was agreed to, unfortunately, I never got there. It was excuses after excuses until I got tired and left it.

On another occasion, I was called by a producer on a lifestyle programme and they wanted me to come coach live on their TV show. It sounded exciting and I was clear from the beginning that I would invoice them. Upon hearing this the producer told me that they had no budget for this, but as always the opportunity was great. This time though, I put my foot down and refused to work for free. After a lot of negotiating, we settled on them covering my travel costs. I was given the brief and had to prepare. On my way there on the day, I filled my car with fuel, and I had an amazing time coaching the team live on set. At the end, I asked for my fuel money. I was told that they were not going to give me cash but were going to use their boss's card and invited me to drive to the fuel station where my fuel would be paid for. Having filled my car with fuel, what I needed was the cash. It took a while to organise but eventually I did get cash to reimburse my fuel.

The key lesson from these two early experiences was to get the agreement in writing, so as to formalise it. Too often when starting out there may be an excitement at landing assignments but unless agreements are written down and formalized, anything can happen.

Exposure is important but it doesn't have to be at the expense of the service provider.

#Iknowthisfosho

**EVEN THOUGH EXPOSURE IS PRECIOUS, IT
DOESN'T HAVE TO BE FREE**

WHAT AN AMBUSH

I have mega respect for network marketing. I know people who do well in that area. I suppose it is proof that whatever that you set your mind on, you can achieve.

What I do not understand and appreciate is the marketing strategy where potential partners and clients are lied to, to get them signed up. I encounter people who are dedicated to convince me that I need to join their business network even when I have indicated that I am not interested. Do they maybe think that I can't think for myself?

I once received a call from a stranger who called me by name, excited after reading about me and my business in a magazine. Fair enough, I thought. She went on to tell me that she would like for us to meet, as she also was a business woman and would like to explore business ideas with me. We engaged in a pleasant discussion and we agreed to find time to meet, explore and share. The following day she called me again to invite me to a meeting with her business associates. I asked what the purpose of the meeting was. She confidently informed me that one of them had just come back from an overseas trip and had interesting business ideas to share. Fantastic, so I thought. This meeting was scheduled.

On the afternoon, just before the meeting, I had some discomfort and anxiety about this meeting. I should have followed my instincts and cancelled. I didn't, I feared being thought of as unprofessional and unnecessarily suspicious. I also feared losing out on a possible opportunity.

Now I know, I should have listened to my instincts. Before I was to leave my house, I wrote down the address and details of where I was going and gave instructions to my family. I made it light hearted as I didn't want them to worry. I was thinking we live in a very unpredictable and unsafe world.

Once the meeting began, it did not take long to for the penny to drop, network marketing! I felt so betrayed, I wanted to leave. I knew the product. There were about 15 – 20 people and about 5 of us were potential recruits. We were seated strategically, inside the circle to make it difficult to leave. So, we sat. The focus was all on us and it was unbearable, unpleasant and undesirable. I really did feel like they were watching my moves, so they know when to "attack" me with the scheme, "kill me" with the opportunity to make loads of money and cook me in the stories of those who were successful in the scheme.

I should have just excused myself and left. A presentation that could have taken fifteen minutes was dragged on for about an hour. I forced a smile and felt so lucky when I left the place after the meeting, I really did.

I did not join and my host took it very personal. So we lose some and win some, as the saying goes.

Two weeks later I was again invited to 'explore a business opportunity'. This was from someone I know, and I was amused by the way she framed the conversation. She said that she knows I love helping others and making money. This time I asked directly and probed as to exactly what the meeting was about, and she evaded the issue, so I asked directly if it was a networking marketing opportunity. Sheepishly, she responded with, "It's not just about selling". Again, a product I knew. I declined and was pleased that I was not tricked into attending.

I am a customer of network marketing products. I have also tried my hand at network marketing. I am appreciative of how I was introduced to the products. There were no secrets or tricks and I was very open minded. I listened and I am now a consumer. I am still curious as to why others prefer to ambush us instead of trick us.

SELLING IS NOT A ONE SIZE FITS ALL. It's easy to lose out on potential partners if you expect all of them to want to be sold to in the same manner.

CORPORATE TOXICITY

I had just started work at this organisation and was feeling strong and militant. I was eager, to change the world, so to speak. As part of my orientation, I must have missed the fact that the leader of the organisation was not to be challenged, that his word was always final. The fact that he would say things and ask leading questions, to which the team responded favourably, agreeing with him, did not in any way render him democratic in his leadership. He sadly thought he was democratic.

We needed him to be present, for an important session we were planning on transformation. I was the organiser and driver for this session and project. It was important for him to be present, as the leader, to set the tone so it would be relatively easier to have the rest of the executive team enrolled. We wanted to foster change from the top, to get buy in from him so it could be easier for others to follow. After a number of engagements on the matter, he agreed, it looked like he understood.

The nature of leadership engagement in some organisations is not robust enough. In such organisations, the leader is dominant, almost dictatorial and not open to be challenged. They sadly don't see themselves that way because no one tells them out of fear, and because they don't accept feedback.

On the day of the planned session, the leader formally welcomed all those present and declared the session opened. He then proceeded to announce that something important had come up for him and he had to go. He glibly just said we would be fine without him. I stood up and challenged him, whilst everybody sat quietly. In hindsight, I could hear the silence from my colleagues. The way they looked at me and tried to warn me with their eyes, unfortunately I did not get the memo that no one questioned or challenged the leader. I imagine how sorry they felt for not briefing me earlier. It was too late!
The lion tore me into pieces, chewed me and spit me out. I was left very disorientated, humiliated and very hurt as he marched out. There was an eerie silence after that. I had to find a way to carry on, and we did carry on. No one said a thing. We pretended that all was fine.

Only once outside of the session, we spoke in hushed tones about what transpired. I did not know then, that I had suffered trauma from that experience. I was silenced for about six to seven years. My fear of speaking out, of voicing a different opinion to people in power became magnified.

The sad thing about corporate trauma, is that we are sometimes not able to identify it whilst we are inside. We carry on thinking it's the demand of the job, fatigue and all the responsibilities put together that renders one in this state. I could not be angry ever again, after that encounter. I was afraid of being angry. A high-ranking white man, with all the trappings of power spoke down to me, an African woman - someone at the very bottom of all rank imaginable - in the presence of other white and black men and women, unchallenged. He purposed to set the record straight and de-mystify any illusion of equality amongst us. I got it.

I crawled back into my cave. I did not know then, that I lost my capacity to be angry. My wings were clipped. It was much later, in my life, long after I had left corporate when I was awakened to my fear of anger. I was able to identify and trace back this fear, to acknowledge the trauma most black women in corporate live through, the trauma of being lorded over by white males. I ached...then I got free. This is a result of continuing to work on myself.

What is now evident, is that I was not the only one silenced with fear. Some in the team were silenced long before I got there. Compliance was safer even though it was costly health wise.

#Iknowthisfosho

The walk of courage is lonely. It is a do or die.
There are no cheer leaders on the side. We are called,
as individuals, to walk the path on our own. It is do -
able. **PRIORITISE SELF-CARE, AS A LEADER**

VIOLENCE AGAINST WOMEN

The painful scourge of violence against women has impacted and continues to affect lives of most women and their families in South Africa. In homes, places of worship and in our communities, abuse of women and children is rife.

I thankfully got employed immediately after I completed my degree. I served as an industrial social worker for a few years before I went full on into a Human Resources role. On the day I was due to attend my graduation ceremony, one of my clients, a fellow colleague, had been physically abused by her husband the night before. He had thrown a hot iron towards her.

Fortunately, she managed to duck and lock herself in another bedroom. There was a history of abuse, which I knew about but this time she was much angrier, and shaken. She wanted to lay a charge against him. I went with her to the Hillbrow police station, as it was the closest to our office.

We waited in the queue for a while. As our turn to go the counter approached, she asked me if her husband was going to get arrested, now that she will be laying a charge against him. I was a bit annoyed with that question and I remember how I responded. I told her yes, it was not for the police to take him on a picnic, but the duty of police is to arrest offenders like her husband. I could see from her body language that she was uncomfortable and having a change of mind, again. We had walked this path before. She murmured something about their daughter, how the arrest would impact her and what if her husband lost his job. She aborted the mission to get her husband arrested because she could not go on with it. I was livid, I had to hide my feelings because it really was her decision, I was there as support.

This happens a lot in instances of women abuse. Some do lay charges and then withdraw them for various reasons. Issues of fear around financial support, social status, and shame are some of the reasons why women do not go ahead with reporting men who violate them.

So, we went back to the office, as I was preparing to leave. She refused to stay at the office or go home. I was too pre-occupied to notice that she was afraid, she was very afraid of going home. I now have an appreciation of her dilemma and her fears. Her husband was a respected man, a church leader and corporate high flyer. He served on several boards of prestigious companies and financially he provided some stability and a good life for the family. She was not going to be able to sustain their lifestyle on her meagre earnings. She was afraid she would have been seen as the one responsible for his downfall, if it ever led to that. She suffered from an inferiority complex, because the husband always told her she was stupid, uneducated and ugly.

I also did not escape abuse.

We met at university and connected like a duck on water. We laughed a lot, enjoyed hearty conversations, walked together and drove around. Lovely guy with a big heart and a big smile, or so I thought.

He started putting out feelers about us getting married. We both were single parents, so we spoke about the children a lot. I was shocked one day, when he told me that my child would have to stay with my parents when we got married because that is his culture: he would not raise another man's child in his own home. This pierced so deep. I looked at his face when he said this, he had a smile that had a wickedness to it, I could not even read his face. I told him categorically that my child will go with me wherever I go. For me, no child meant no marriage.

He was taken aback, thinking about it now, he probably expected me to agree, or to negotiate. Even though I did want to get married to him at the time, it was never going to be at my child's expense. Both my parents were alive and they were taking care of my child as I was at university full time. The arrangement I had with them was that I would resume the responsibility after completing my degree.
So now here was this man, who I thought cared about me, with great prospects, pledging his love for me, and at the same time, not extending the same love to my child. We both are African and for the life of me, it was the first time that I heard about

that culture.

We continued to see each other, but something had shifted. Then the abuse started. He would calmly put me down, tell me that I am not as smart as I want others to believe. It was so subtle, he would say one hurtful thing and then invite me out for coffee, or a walk and it seemed all normal. I always had issues with my body and sometimes he would say one unkind thing about my body, and he would hug me and tell me he appreciates me. I was so confused, and I tried to hide my confusion to my friends who thought I had scored a great guy. He was a great conversationalist, smart, witty and good looking, what more would a girl want? I kept having moments of self-doubt, believing everything he was saying about me.

One day I had a visit from a guy friend I had not seen in a long time. I introduced them to each other and the three of us spent some time together. My boyfriend then had to leave. When he got back, my friend had already left. He was angry about my friend. I was shocked because he seemed fine earlier. He accused me of having an affair with my friend and he slapped me. I knew that it was the end of this relationship.

I almost married this man. If it was not for the fact that I had a child. The shock would probably had come with me inside marriage. Every time I think about this, I am truly grateful I did not marry him. The thing is he had started breaking me down and I possibly could not have felt empowered enough to leave, after marriage.
After him, I was in a relationship with another abuser. Very

sophisticated and traditional, using culture to oppress. I did not see that in him at the time. He was gregarious, very confident and aware of himself. He was very protective and had a softness combined with toughness that was truly attractive. We came from a similar background and I thought he was it. We had a disagreement one day, and he slapped me real hard. He then embraced me and softly told me there would be more if I didn't toe the line. I immediately went to my parents and told them. My mother called him immediately and when hearing my mother's voice on the phone, he dropped the call. My mother was livid, and he knew he could not mess with me any further. He apologised.

We continued seeing each other and for a long time there was no abuse, even though unnecessary disagreements would be there. Then the abuse started again, fiercely. One day he threatened me in front of my friends and told them to mind their own business. They were shocked and felt powerless and I realised at that time that he had nothing to lose. He would wait for me after work, just so I knew 'he was in charge'. I felt helpless because I had lied to my folks. I had told them that I was not seeing him anymore. Whenever I tried to end the relationship with him, he threatened me. I should have remembered how non-judgemental my folks were and I did not want any situation where my father got involved, because he would.

I eventually told my folks and there was no turning back. Thank God I was eventually able to leave him. I told him it was over, for real. I had uttered those words before but I knew this time it was for ever. I had cast my thoughts and visualised a future with this man and all I saw were images of me pregnant and barefoot. I had become fearful of him and I knew love and fear can never exist together.

I also knew my parents would not always be around, and that I would have no one to protect me. This decision came from my mouth and all of my body and somehow he got it.

The shame of abuse is what made me not talk about it. I hardly ever share this part of my life because I used to think that I don't fit the stereotype. Today I know that I do. I'm a woman and sadly my story is not unique, it merely highlights how anyone can be vulnerable. We live in a country where women are beaten, raped and killed. I am grateful to be alive.

#Iknowthisfosho

I fit the profile of an abused woman
Rich, poor, educated, un-educated, young, old.
As a woman who suffered abuse, *I AM NOT RESPONSIBLE
FOR THE ACTIONS OF THE MEN WHO ABUSED ME.* I am
strong and powerful. The first time he abuses you, don't
ignore it, don't become seduced by his gifts and apologies.
Do yourself a favour, leave.

———————————————